CONSTRUCTION OPTIMIZATION

11 STRATEGIES FOR 30% COST SAVINGS AND 20% TIME REDUCTION

CONSTRUCTION OPTIMIZATION

11 STRATEGIES FOR 30% COST SAVINGS AND 20% TIME REDUCTION

Sharad Gupta

Worldwide Published by
Pendown Press

PENDOWN PRESS LLP

An ISO 9001 & ISO 14001 Certified Co.,

Regd. Office: 3767A, Kanhaiya Nagar,

Tri Nagar, Delhi-110035

Ph.: 8130886000, 9650072927, 8595249536

E-mail: info@pendownpress.com

Branch Office: 1A/2A, 20, Hari Sadan, Ansari Road,

Daryaganj, New Delhi-110002

Ph.: 011-45794768

Website: PendownPress.com

Edition: 2024

Price: ₹ 399/-

ISBN: 978-93-5554-758-3

Layout and Cover Designed by Pendown Graphics Team
Printed and Bound in India by Thomson Press India Ltd.

Imagine this...

you're a property owner, eagerly envisioning your dream office or factory taking shape. You've poured your heart and soul into the design, imagining the perfect space where innovation thrives and productivity soars. However, as construction kicks off, you're hit with a barrage of unexpected challenges.

Budgets skyrocket due to unforeseen structural issues, and your dream project faces delays, pushing your timeline further and further back. You're overwhelmed, frustrated, and unsure how to proceed. You thought you had everything planned, but now you're facing a mountain of problems you never anticipated.

Seeking guidance, you turn to consultants, hoping they can help steer you back on track. But their fees add up, stretching your budget even thinner. It feels like every step forward is met with two steps back, and you're left wondering if your dream will ever become a reality.

This is a reality many property owners face in the world of civil work. The emotional toll of watching your vision falter, the stress of financial strain, and the uncertainty of what lies ahead can be crushing. But there is a glimmer of hope.

With my 25 years of experience in Design and Structure, I'm here to guide you through these challenges. Together, we can navigate the complexities of civil work, avoid common pitfalls, and turn your dream into a reality. Let's work together to build a space that not only meets your expectations but exceeds them.

Introduction

Hello, my name is Sharad Gupta. I have been working as a Structural Consultant and Civil Contractor for the past 25 years. Throughout my professional journey, I have observed the need for a high level of professionalism in the construction industry.

In the early stages of my career as a Civil Engineer, I found it challenging to sustain a meaningful professional life beyond 2 to 3 years. Recognizing the complexities in construction and inspired to contribute to my country and industry, I transitioned into becoming a contractor. My goal was to provide the best quality work based on my knowledge and contribute positively to the industry I am passionate about.

After 25 years of dedicated service to my clients, I decided to venture into managing construction projects myself. I witnessed numerous projects I had designed deteriorating within 15 to 20 years due to subpar construction quality, leading to significant consequences and financial losses. Understanding that the structure is the backbone of any building, I realized that the overall cost of a building is only about 25% of the tool cost, with the quality of construction accounting for a mere 5%. However, this small percentage has a profound impact on the entire lifespan of the building. If construction is compromised, it becomes complicated, especially when occupants are already living in the building.

In today's scenario, clients often opt for cost-effective solutions without considering the true cost of construction. This often leads to the hiring of substandard contractors, resulting in compromised quality.

My advice to building owners is to select a contractor not solely based on the lowest bid but to conduct a proper rate analysis before finalizing. In my book, I have outlined 11 recommendations that, if implemented, can save 20% in both time and money for overall projects.

I am on a mission to elevate mid-level construction quality to the highest standards, ensuring the safety of buildings for 50-75 years. If you have any questions or need assistance with these solutions or any other construction-related queries, I am more than happy to help you save both time and money.

Contents

My Story

Mr. Sharad Gupta

Founder and Director, Sanrachna Project India Pvt. Ltd.

My name is Sharad Gupta, and I am from Madhya Pradesh. My family has traditionally been in the service sector, but during my upbringing, I was always fascinated by the business community. Growing up, I aspired to be a self-made businessman. Initially, after graduating, I took up small-time jobs to make ends meet, but I found it challenging to sustain those jobs for extended periods.

Consequently, I decided to start my own venture with two people. However, it didn't take long for me to realize that the construction sector is highly unorganized and filled with individuals lacking technical qualifications to understand the complexity and importance of the industry. Despite contributing about 8-10% towards the nation's GDP, the construction industry remains disorganized.

I have been involved in the construction industry for over 20 years and have made it a priority to educate clients for a better and more efficient process. This approach benefits both the clients and the nation, fostering simultaneous growth.

DISCLAIMER

In all our case studies, we implement a rigorous approach to safeguard the confidentiality of our clients. As a standard practice, we discreetly alter the names and locations featured in our case study narratives. This careful process lets us share important insights into our successful projects while keeping sensitive information private. Our commitment to client privacy is paramount, and this precautionary measure reflects our dedication to maintaining the highest ethical standards in our work.

Who is This For?

This is for those Who
Want to Construct
New Factory Building.

AGENDA

Description of the **11 Steps** to **Reduce the Cost and Timing** of Upcoming Factory Construction.

Testimonials

> **M/s Sanrachna Solutions LLP, led by Sharad Gupta, is a professional and dedicated organization.**
>
> They delivered our school within the record time of 9 months despite facing a lot of challenges. His team is also completely dedicated to their work.
>
> **Dr. Michael Williams**
> Director Mount Carmel School

Testimonials

Testimonials

M/s Sanrachna Solutions LLP (Sharad Gupta) is a proficient organization consistently achieving remarkable quality in concrete and brickwork using standard shuttering and bricks.

Mrs. Bharti Batra

Director Prakriti School

List of Few Clients

Certificates

CHIEF TOWN & COUNTRY PLANNER
TOWN AND COUNTRY PLANNING DEPARTMENT
GOVERNMENT OF UTTARAKHAND
5ᵗʰ Floor, Rajiv Gandhi Multipurpose Complex, Dispensary Road, Dehradun-248001

CERTIFICATE
for
STATE LEVEL STRUCTURE ENGINEER REGISTRATION
IN TOWN AND COUNTRY PLANNING DEPARTMENT
Registration No. DoH-UK/ G-I / ASE- 19/2022

*Certified that **Er. Sharad Gupta** S/o Sh. Ramesh Prasad Gupta, office address: C-903, Himachali C.G.H.S. Plot No. 8, sec-3, Dwarka here by Registered as a **State Level Structure Engineer** in **'Grade-I'** for the state of Uttarakhand as per the Uttarakhand Bhawan Nirman Evam Vikas Upvidhi-2011(Amended) vide Government Notification No.837/v-2-2016-127(aa.)/15-T.C. Dated: 03.06.2016 with the conditions given below:*

1. The buildings designed by the Registered Structure Engineer will be audited by Town and Country Planning Department on half yearly basis.

2. The Registered Structure Engineer will compulsorily provide the information regarding the certified structural design by E-mail on ctcpase@gmail.com or by themself representative every two months, or else the certificate will be deemed cancelled.

3. The Registered Structure Engineer will comply the duties and responsibilities given inAnnexure-5 of the Building Byelaws. The Structure Engineer shall provide the information regarding completion of development work by the applicant to the Town and Country Planning Department/ Concerned Development Authority.

4. Applicant and the Registered Structure Engineer shall be jointly responsible for the construction of the building as per structural design and the structural safety of the constructed building.

Validity of the empanelment: Three years from the date of issuing of the certificate.

Date: 17-12-2022

(Shashi Mohan Srivastava)
Chief Town & Country Planner/ Senior Planner,
Town & Country Planning Department,
Dehradun

X

Certificates

Certificates

Certificates

PE7006743

The Institution of Engineers (India)

By virtue of expertise in the profession of engineering
in the field of Civil Engineering

Sharad Gupta

is hereby authorised to use the style and title of

Professional Engineer (India)

This certificate is valid upto

31st August 2028

In witness whereof the said Institution has
caused its Common Seal to be affixed this

4th August 2023

8 Gokhale Road
Kolkata - 700 020, India

Secretary & Director General

President

Chapter-1

The Risks of Appointing Inadequate and Inefficient Consultants

Story for Chapter 1

Once upon a time, in the bustling city of Nagpur, there lived a young entrepreneur named Maya. Maya had a dream of building her own factory, a place where she could bring her innovative ideas to life and create a product that would revolutionize the market.

Excited and full of ambition, Maya set out to find the perfect consultants to help her turn her dream into reality. However, in her eagerness to get started, Maya made a common mistake – she appointed consultants based solely on their low fees, without considering their qualifications or track record.

As the project progressed, Maya began to notice red flags. The consultants seemed disorganized and often missed deadlines. The quality of their work was subpar, leading to frequent errors and rework. Despite these warning signs, Maya continued to work with them, hoping that things would improve.

Unfortunately, things only got worse. The consultants' inefficiency led to delays in the project timeline, causing costs to escalate. Maya's dream was slowly turning into a nightmare as she struggled to keep the project on track and within budget.

One day, Maya received devastating news – the consultants had made a critical error in their calculations, leading to a major structural flaw in the building. The project would need to be halted, and significant repairs would be required, costing Maya both time and money.

Heartbroken and disappointed, Maya realized the true cost of appointing inadequate and inefficient consultants. She had cut corners in an attempt to save money, but in the end, it had cost her dearly. Her dream lay in ruins, all because she had not taken the time to find the right consultants for the job.

Maya's story serves as a cautionary tale for all aspiring entrepreneurs. The risks of appointing inadequate consultants are real and can have far-reaching consequences. It's essential to do thorough research and choose consultants based on their expertise and track record, rather than their fees alone. After all, when it comes to turning dreams into reality, shortcuts are never the answer.

Inadequate and Inefficient Consultants

With Consultant

Each consultant plays a crucial role in the architectural process, contributing their expertise to different aspects of a construction project. Here's a breakdown of the major role of each consultant:

a. **Soil Consultant:**

- **Major Role:** Assessing and analyzing the soil conditions at the construction site.

- **Responsibilities:**

    - Conducting soil tests to determine soil composition, strength, and stability.

    - Providing recommendations for foundation design based on soil properties.

    - Advising on potential soil-related challenges and proposing mitigation measures.

b. **Architect:**

- **Major Role:** Designing the overall structure, appearance, and functionality of the building.

- **Responsibilities:**

    - Creating architectural drawings and plans.

    - Collaborating with clients to understand their needs and preferences.

    - Ensuring compliance with building codes and regulations.

- Overseeing the aesthetic and functional aspects of the project.

c. **Structure Consultant:**

- **Major Role:** Designing the structural elements of the building to ensure stability and safety.

- **Responsibilities:**

  - Developing structural plans and calculations.

  - Selecting appropriate materials for construction.

  - Ensuring that the building can withstand loads and environmental conditions.

  - Collaborating with the architect to integrate structural elements into the design.

d. **MEP Consultant (Mechanical, Electrical, Plumbing):**

- **Major Role:** Designing the mechanical, electrical, and plumbing systems of the building.

- **Responsibilities:**

  - Planning and designing HVAC (Heating, Ventilation, and Air Conditioning) systems.

  - Designing electrical systems, including lighting and power distribution.

  - Planning plumbing and fire protection systems.

  - Ensuring energy efficiency and compliance with codes.

e. **Project Management Consultant:**

- **Major Role:** Overseeing the project from initiation to completion, ensuring it is delivered on time and within budget.

- **Responsibilities:**
  - Developing project schedules and budgets.
  - Coordinating communication among various stakeholders.
  - Monitoring project progress and addressing any issues.
  - Managing risks and implementing mitigation strategies.
  - Ensuring compliance with regulations and quality standards.

In summary, each consultant brings specialized knowledge to the construction project, contributing to a comprehensive and well-executed architectural design. Their collaboration is essential for the successful completion of a building project.

Without Consultants

The absence or neglect of any of these consultants can have significant negative impacts on architectural work and the overall construction project. Here's a breakdown of the potential consequences:

a. **Soil Consultant:**

-   **Without:**

    -   Risk of inadequate foundation design.

    -   Increased susceptibility to soil-related issues such as settlement, instability, or erosion.

    -   Potential for structural failure due to poor soil conditions.

b. **Architect:**

-   **Without:**

    -   Lack of a comprehensive and well-designed building plan.

    -   Aesthetic and functional issues in the final structure.

    -   Non-compliance with building codes and regulations.

    -   Increased likelihood of redesign during construction, leading to delays and extra costs.

c. **Structure Consultant:**

-   **Without**

    -   Higher risk of structural instability and failure.

    -   Inefficient use of materials, potentially leading to increased costs.

    -   Difficulty integrating structural elements with the overall architectural design.

    -   Greater susceptibility to structural problems during construction.

d. **MEP Consultant (Mechanical, Electrical, Plumbing):**

- **Without:**

  - Inadequate or inefficient HVAC, electrical, and plumbing systems.

  - Increased energy consumption and operational costs.

  - Reduced occupant comfort and safety.

  - Challenges in coordinating MEP systems with the overall building design.

e. **Project Management Consultant:**

- **Without:**

  - Lack of proper planning, leading to delays and budget overruns.

  - Poor communication and coordination among project stakeholders.

  - Increased likelihood of disputes and conflicts during construction.

  - Difficulty in managing risks and implementing timely solutions to issues.

In summary, the absence of any of these consultants can result in compromised structural integrity, functionality, aesthetics, and overall project management. Collaboration among these professionals is essential for a successful architectural project, ensuring that it meets design requirements, complies with regulations, and is delivered on time and within budget.

Conclusion

While appointing all the mentioned consultants adds an upfront cost to the project and may extend the timeline, it is crucial to recognize that their roles are essential for the successful execution of architectural work. The 30% to 40% increase in time and money spent can be viewed as an investment in ensuring the project's quality, safety, and adherence to regulations. Neglecting these consultants might lead to even greater costs in the long run due to potential issues, redesigns, and construction problems. So, although it might seem like more money and time now, in the long run, it ensures a well-planned, compliant, and sturdy construction project.

O   O   O   O

Case Study (1) of Inadequate and Inefficient Consultants

One of our clients, Mr. Siddharth Gupta, constructed a factory in Hapur, Uttar Pradesh. He appointed two major consultants for structural and architectural aspects but did not engage an MEP consultant. He believed that the MEP consultant's responsibilities could be managed based on our experience. Unfortunately, during the construction, the entire building was raised to the level of the external road, covering a total factory area of 5 acres. The construction followed standard procedures as per local plumbing norms, resulting in the creation of eight water harvesting pits, each costing Rs. 20 Lakhs, with a total expenditure of Rs. 1.60 Crores.

After the first rainfall, all the water harvesting pits were found to be choked. Subsequently, a plumbing consultant was hired to investigate the issue. The consultant discovered that the natural water level was too high, preventing water from reaching the harvesting pits. To address this, a 1.5 lakh-liter water tank was installed to prevent temporary flooding in the factory area. Excess water was directed to the sewage area. This experience highlights the importance of engaging professional consultants to avoid such conditions and emphasizes the value of investing in expertise for a smoother construction process.

The Unseen Costs of Unprofessional Contractor Appointments

Story for Chapter 2

In the lively city of Gurgaon, the Guptas, who had been saving money for a long time, started building their dream home with excitement. They hired a contractor who offered them a good deal, beginning this exciting new phase of their lives.

At first, everything seemed to be going well. The contractor assured them that the project would be completed quickly and within their budget. However, as the construction progressed, the Guptas started noticing problems.

The contractor and his team were often careless and sloppy. They used poor quality materials and ignored safety regulations. The Guptas became increasingly worried, but they didn't want to stop the construction and delay their dream home.

As a result, the construction was completed, but it was far from perfect. There were several issues that needed to be fixed, and the Guptas had to spend more money than they had planned for. They realized that the true cost of hiring an unprofessional contractor far exceeded their expectations.

The Guptas were disappointed and frustrated. They had worked so hard to save up for their dream home, only to have it marred by the mistakes of an unprofessional contractor. They wished they had done more research and chosen a contractor who was more reliable and experienced.

In the end, the Guptas learned an important lesson - that the unseen costs of hiring an unprofessional contractor can be devastating. It's not just about the money, but also about the emotional toll it takes. They vowed to be more careful in the future and to always prioritize quality over cost.

Contractor Professional Vs Unprofessional

A. **Quality of Work:**

- **Professional:** Prioritizes quality construction, follows industry standards, and ensures work meets or exceeds specifications.

- **Unprofessional:** Work quality may be subpar, with shortcuts taken that compromise the integrity of the structure.

B. **Reliability and Timeliness:**

- **Professional:** Consistently meets project deadlines and delivers work on time. Demonstrates reliability in project completion.

- **Unprofessional:** Often experiences delays, lacks punctuality, and may not fulfill contractual obligations on schedule.

C. **Client References:**

- **Professional:** Can provide positive references from satisfied clients and has a reputation for delivering successful projects.

- **Unprofessional:** May lack positive references or could have a history of client dissatisfaction.

D. **Safety Practices:**

- **Professional:** Prioritizes safety on the construction site, implements proper safety measures, and conducts regular safety training.

- **Unprofessional:** May neglect safety protocols, putting workers and the project at risk of accidents and injuries.

E. **Contractual Transparency:**

- **Professional:** Clearly outlines project scope, costs, and terms in the contract. Ensures transparency in all financial transactions.

- **Unprofessional:** Contracts may be vague or lack transparency, leading to disputes and disagreements during the project.

Overall, choosing a professional civil contractor is crucial for the success of any construction project, as it ensures a higher likelihood of timely completion, quality work, and adherence to safety and regulatory standards.

Conclusion

In conclusion, while it is true that hiring a professional civil contractor may lead to higher costs, the investment is justified by the invaluable benefits they bring to a construction project. The expertise, experience, and commitment to quality work offered by professional contractors outweigh the potential short-term savings associated with unprofessional counterparts. Professional contractors contribute to the success of a project by ensuring adherence to regulations, maintaining high safety standards, providing transparent communication, and delivering work on time and within budget. Choosing a professional civil contractor is an essential strategic decision that fosters the efficient and successful completion of construction endeavors, ultimately saving clients from potential long-term costs and complications.

Case Study (2) of
Unprofessional Contractor Appointments

One esteemed client, Siddharth International School, located in Noida, Uttar Pradesh, appointed an unprofessional contractor for the construction of their school building. During the excavation in Noida, we discovered Yamuna sand. To profit from selling the sand, the contractor excavated the soil an additional 600 mm beyond the required depth. The very next day, the main contractor became aware of the issue, but due to a lack of knowledge, he backfilled the soil and used a compactor to compact it, proceeding with the construction of a 4-story building.

After three years, the building developed major cracks, prompting an investigation by a professional consultant. The consultant determined that the overall design of the building was satisfactory, but the foundation had settled in locations with higher loads. This emphasizes the importance of appointing a professional contractor with a civil engineering background to avoid such mishaps. A similar incident occurred in Dwarka, where nearly 500 societies faced issues because the contractor used salty water.

Although the cost of water in the overall construction is less than 0.5 percent, it can significantly damage buildings, reducing their lifespan by almost 50%. It underscores the critical need to ensure the quality of construction materials and practices for the long-term durability of structures.

CHAPTER-3

The Art and Importance of Proper Drawing Management

Story for Chapter 3

In the bustling metropolis of Delhi/NCR, there was a young architect named Raj, who had a passion for creating beautiful buildings that stood the test of time. Raj understood the importance of proper drawing management in his projects and approached his work with meticulous attention to detail.

Raj had witnessed many projects suffer due to poor drawing management. Clients would often make changes to the original drawings without proper documentation, leading to confusion and errors during construction. This resulted in delays and increased costs, much to the frustration of everyone involved.

Determined to avoid these pitfalls, Raj made sure to keep detailed records of all drawings and changes made throughout the project. He maintained clear communication with his clients and contractors, ensuring that everyone was on the same page.

One day, Raj was approached by a client who wanted to make a significant change to the design of their building. Thanks to Raj's careful drawing management, he was able to quickly assess the impact of the change and provide a revised drawing that satisfied the client's requirements without compromising the integrity of the design.

Impressed by Raj's professionalism and attention to detail, the client praised him for his work. The project was completed on time and within budget, bringing much delight to everyone involved.

Raj's story serves as a reminder of the importance of proper drawing management in construction projects. By maintaining detailed records and ensuring clear communication, architects and designers can ensure that their projects are successful and free from costly errors.

Improper drawing management

Improper drawing management without revisions in a construction project can lead to a range of consequences, affecting various aspects of the project. Here are some potential outcomes:

A. Design Inconsistencies:

- **Consequence:** Without proper drawing management, discrepancies and inconsistencies may arise between different versions of drawings. This can cause confusion among construction teams and subcontractors, leading to errors in the implementation of the design.

B. **Construction Errors:**

- **Consequence:** Outdated drawings may lead construction teams to work with incorrect or obsolete information. This can result in errors during the building process, such as incorrect placement of structural elements, improper installation of systems, or other construction defects.

C. **Cost Overruns:**

- **Consequence:** Construction errors and rework due to outdated drawings can result in additional costs. Contractors may need to spend extra time and resources to rectify mistakes, leading to budget overruns and financial strain on the project.

D. **Project Delays:**

- **Consequence:** Inconsistent or outdated drawings can cause delays as construction teams may need to pause work to clarify discrepancies or wait for revised drawings. This can extend the project timeline and affect overall project delivery.

E. **Client Dissatisfaction:**

- **Consequence:** Clients may be dissatisfied with the final result if the construction deviates from the intended design due to improper drawing management. This dissatisfaction can harm the contractor's reputation and lead to disputes.

Conclusion

During the project, drawings ranging from 1 to 100 are received from various consultants, each designated for different purposes such as "good for construction," "for approval," or "for reference only." This diversity in modes of submission poses challenges for the Project Management Consultant (PMC) and the site execution team. To streamline communication and avoid potential issues, it is recommended to establish a centralized point for managing all types of drawings from different consultants.

To address this, a Google link will be created, adhering to the specified format below. Consultants are required to upload their AutoCAD and PDF format drawings to this link. The contents of this link will then be shared with all stakeholders, including the PMC, contractor, clients, and consultants. It is important to note that only the final approved drawings will be followed for implementation.

Case Study (3) of Proper Drawing Management

In Ahmedabad, Gujarat, Siddhartha Steel Ltd, one of our clients, experienced significant changes in their team of consultants and PMC during the COVID-19 pandemic. We received more than 400 drawings from various consultants to initiate our work. After the pandemic, it took almost two months with the assistance of five qualified consultants to organize the drawings in a sequential manner, enabling us to kick-start our operations at full capacity. This was necessary as many contractors exploit revised drawings for their advantage.

Recognizing the challenges posed by improper drawing management, where contractors often impose extra charges, we implemented a standardized format for drawing management. This format has proven to be highly effective, and has been consistently applied across all our projects, benefiting both our team and our clients.

Chart of Drawing Management

SANRACHNA SOLUTIONS LLP

PROJECT:	30 6 - Residence, Kokapet, Hyderabad				CATEGORY - As per customer requirement or as below											REV.NO.	0
CLIENT:	Sriram Group				D - Detail Design Drawing						P - Preliminary					DATE	06-10-2023
ARCHITECT:	DA Studios Private Limited				A - Approval		M - FEM Analysis Model				I - Information						
PROJECT CODE :	253103	Title:	Cost In Site Drawings		B - As-built						G - Good for Construction / Production						

SR.NO.	DRG. / DOC. No.	DESCRIPTION	DRG. SIZE	CAT.		REV. 0	Link of File	REV. 1	Link of File	RE 2	Link of File	REV. 3	Link of File	REV. 4	Link of File	REV. 5	REV. 6	Remarks
		List of Drawings																
		STRUCTURE DRAWING																
1	SEPL-SGH-KKP-ST-001	Cover Sheet	A1	G	Sub Date	15-09-2023		23-09-2023										
2	SEPL-SGH-KKP-ST-002	Drawing index	A1	G	Sub Date	15-09-2023		23-09-2023										
3	SEPL-SGH-KKP-ST-003	General Notes & Details (1)	A1	G	Sub Date	15-09-2023	Z-02 SANRACHN	05-10-2023										
4	SEPL-SGH-KKP-ST-004	General Notes & Details (2)	A1	G	Sub Date	15-09-2023	Z-02											
5	SEPL-SGH-KKP-ST-005	General Notes & Details (3)	A1	G	Sub Date	15-09-2023	Z-02											
6	SEPL-SGH-KKP-ST-006	General Notes & Details (4)	A1	G	Sub Date	15-09-2024	Z-02											
7	SEPL-SGH-KKP-ST-100	PCC Layout	A1	G	Sub Date	14-09-2023		23-09-2023										
8	SEPL-SGH-KKP-ST-101	Foundation Layout	A1	G	Sub Date	15-09-2023		23-09-2023		05-10-2023								
9	SEPL-SGH-KKP-ST-102	Foundation Bottom Reinforcement	A1	G	Sub Date	23-09-2023		05-10-2023										
10	SEPL-SGH-KKP-ST-103	Foundation Top Reinforcement	A1	G	Sub Date	23-09-2023		05-10-2023										
11	SEPL-SGH-KKP-ST-104	Column & Wall Layout	A1	G	Sub Date	15-09-2023		05-10-2023										
12	SEPL-SGH-KKP-ST-105	Column & Wall Rebar (1)	A1	G	Sub Date	23-09-2023		05-10-2023										
13	SEPL-SGH-KKP-ST-106	Column & Wall Rebar (2)	A1	G	Sub Date	23-09-2023		05-10-2023										
14	SEPL-SGH-KKP-ST-107	Column & Wall Rebar (3)	A1	G	Sub Date	23-09-2023		05-10-2023										
15	SEPL-SGH-KKP-ST-108	Column & Wall Rebar (4)	A1	G	Sub Date	23-09-2023		05-10-2023										
16	SEPL-SGH-KKP-ST-300	Sections (1)	A1	G	Sub Date	23-09-2023		06-10-2023										
17	SEPL-SGH-KKP-ST-301	Sections (2)	A1	G	Sub Date	23-09-2023		06-10-2023										
					Sub Date												
					Sub Date												
					Sub Date												
					Sub Date												
					Sub Date												

CHAPTER-4

Hidden Costs of Improper Quality Management

Story for Chapter 4

In the peaceful town of Sonipat, there lived a builder named Ramesh, known for his unwavering commitment to quality. Ramesh firmly believed that using the best materials and following strict quality standards were essential to building lasting structures.

One day, Ramesh was approached by a client who wanted to construct a residential complex. The client was keen on cutting costs and suggested using cheaper materials to save money. Despite the client's insistence, Ramesh stood firm in his belief that compromising on quality was not an option.

As the construction progressed, Ramesh's decision to prioritize quality became evident. The structures he built stood strong and sturdy, even in the face of harsh weather conditions. Meanwhile, other buildings in the area, constructed using substandard materials, began to show signs of wear and tear.

Years passed, and Ramesh's buildings remained in excellent condition, attracting more clients who valued quality over cost. On the other hand, the buildings constructed using cheaper materials required frequent repairs and maintenance, costing their owners significantly more in the long run.

Ramesh's commitment to quality had not only saved his clients money but had also earned him a reputation as a builder who could be trusted to deliver lasting and reliable structures.

The story of Ramesh serves as a powerful reminder of the hidden costs of compromising on quality. While cutting corners may seem like a way to save money in the short term, the long-term consequences can be far more costly. In the end, investing in quality is an investment in the future.

A. Increased Costs:

- **Details:** Poor quality can result in defects and rework, leading to increased material and labor costs.

- **Solution:** Implement quality control processes to detect defects early, invest in employee training, and use advanced technologies for more efficient and accurate production.

B. Schedule Delays:

- **Details:** Fixing defects and reworking can disrupt project timelines, causing delays in overall completion.

- **Solution:** Develop a comprehensive quality plan, schedule regular inspections, and address issues promptly to minimize disruptions and maintain project timelines.

C. Customer Dissatisfaction:

- **Details:** Low-quality products or services can lead to dissatisfaction, negative reviews, and damage to the company's reputation.

- **Solution:** Establish clear communication channels, set realistic expectations, actively seek customer feedback, and prioritize continuous improvement to enhance customer satisfaction.

D. Risk of Accidents or Failures:

- **Details:** In industries like construction or manufacturing, poor quality may lead to safety hazards, accidents, or structural failures.

- **Solution:** Prioritize safety standards, conduct regular risk assessments, and ensure compliance with industry regulations to minimize the risk of accidents or failures.

E. Resource Wastage:

- **Details:** Inefficient processes and poor quality can lead to wasted materials, labor, and time.

- **Solution:** Optimize processes, invest in employee training programs, and monitor resource usage to reduce waste and enhance efficiency.

F. Loss of Competitive Advantage:

- **Details:** Delivering low-quality products or services can lead to a loss of competitiveness in the market.

- **Solution:** Differentiate the organization by consistently delivering high-quality offerings, actively promote a commitment to quality in marketing efforts, and leveraging positive customer testimonials to showcase reliability and excellence.

G. Difficulty in Continuous Improvement:

- **Details:** Without a focus on quality management, it becomes challenging to implement continuous improvement initiatives.

- **Solution:** Establish a culture of continuous improvement, encourage employee feedback, regularly review and update processes, and invest in technologies that support ongoing enhancements to ensure sustained improvement in quality and efficiency.

Conclusion

In conclusion, the adoption of a comprehensive construction manual by all consultants represents a pivotal step towards ensuring quality control and preventing potential issues in construction projects. Through detailed processes for each activity along with thorough checklists, consultants contribute to a systematic approach that minimizes the risk of improper quality.

This proactive measure addresses various aspects of construction, including structural integrity, quality consistency, adherence to schedules, cost management, and safety. The construction manual serves as a valuable guide for contractors, offering clarity on approved methodologies and promoting standardized practices. The inclusion of checklists further enhances accountability and facilitates a streamlined quality assurance process.

Furthermore, the construction manual not only mitigates the likelihood of structural issues and aesthetic inconsistencies but also contributes to improved project efficiency and reduced costs. It fosters a collaborative environment among stakeholders, emphasizing the importance of adherence to industry standards and regulations. Additionally, the manual serves as a valuable reference point for contractual agreements, reducing the potential for disputes and promoting smoother project execution.

Ultimately, the proactive approach of consultants in providing a construction manual establishes a foundation for excellence, emphasizing a commitment to delivering high-quality outcomes while minimizing the impact of unforeseen challenges. This comprehensive guidance enhances the overall project management process, instilling confidence in stakeholders and contributing to the successful and timely completion of construction endeavors.

○ ○ ○ ○

Case Study (4) of Improper Quality Management

One of our clients, Ms. Palak Gupta, the CEO of a top 10 Indian company, resides in Faridabad, Haryana. After the first wave of COVID-19, she gifted her 82-year-old father, a renowned surgeon, a grand house. The construction was in full swing, but due to quality mismanagement, the contractor sourced plaster sand from a supplier during the rainy season. Unfortunately, the sand had a silt content of more than 20%. After completing the plastering, the civil contractor handed over the site to the interior team.

Upon beginning their work, the interior team discovered that all the plaster had come off due to the high silt content. Consequently, the contractor had to remove all the plaster, leading to a three-month delay in the project to rectify and reapply the plaster. A similar issue occurred with the Italian stone used in the construction. The stone had a fiber film on the back side, and due to improper communication, the contractor did not remove the film. After laying three crores worth of stone, a significant sound emerged during the polishing process. Consequently, all the stones had to be removed, incurring both time and financial costs. Overall, the project experienced a delay of almost 12 months.

CHAPTER-5

The Impact of Unspecified Construction Techniques

Story for Chapter 5

Amidst the hustle and bustle of Pune, there was a young engineer named Anuj who was passionate about construction. Anuj understood the critical importance of using the right construction techniques to ensure the durability and safety of buildings.

One day, Anuj was hired to oversee the construction of a new office building. The client was eager to save money and insisted on using unspecified construction techniques to cut costs. Despite Anuj's warnings about the potential risks, the client remained adamant.

As the construction progressed, the impact of using unspecified construction techniques became evident. The building started to show signs of instability, with cracks appearing in the walls and floors. Anuj knew that if the issues were not addressed promptly, the building could become unsafe for occupancy.

Taking matters into his own hands, Anuj consulted with experts and devised a plan to reinforce the building's structure using the right techniques. Although it was a challenging and costly process, Anuj was determined to ensure the safety of the building and its occupants.

After weeks of hard work, the building was finally deemed safe for occupancy. The client, relieved and grateful, recognized the importance of using specified construction techniques. They thanked Anuj for his dedication and expertise, realizing that cutting corners was not worth the risk.

Anuj's story serves as a valuable lesson for all involved in construction projects. Using the right construction techniques is essential for ensuring the safety and longevity of buildings. Cutting costs may seem tempting, but the long-term consequences can be severe. In the end, investing in the right techniques is an investment in the future.

Unspecified Construction Techniques

A. **Structural Integrity Issues:**

- **Consequences:** Lack of specified construction techniques may lead to compromised structural integrity, posing safety risks, potential building failures, and necessitating costly repairs.

- **Solutions:** Engage structural engineers to provide detailed specifications for construction techniques. Clearly communicate approved methods in project documentation and collaborate closely with contractors to ensure compliance.

B. **Quality Variability:**

- **Consequences:** Unspecified construction techniques can result in inconsistent quality, leading to defects, rework, and disputes with contractors over expectations.

- **Solutions:** Develop comprehensive construction guidelines and standards specifying techniques. Implement regular quality control inspections to ensure adherence to specifications. Provide training to contractors on approved methods.

C. **Schedule Delays:**

- **Consequences:** Construction delays may occur due to uncertainties in methodologies, causing confusion among contractors and workers.

- **Solutions:** Clearly define construction methodologies in project plans. Conduct pre-construction meetings to ensure alignment among all stakeholders. Provide detailed instructions to contractors and address any ambiguities promptly.

D. **Increased Costs:**

- **Consequences:** Unspecified techniques may lead to inefficiencies, errors, and the need for corrective measures, resulting in higher project costs.

- **Solutions:** Conduct a thorough analysis of construction methods during the planning phase. Estimate costs accurately and provide clear guidelines to minimize the risk of budget overruns. Foster open communication to address cost concerns promptly.

E. Contractual Disputes:

- **Consequences:** Ambiguities in construction techniques may lead to disputes between project stakeholders, impacting timelines and relationships.

- **Solutions:** Clearly define construction methods in contracts. Establish dispute resolution mechanisms. Encourage open communication and regular project updates to address concerns promptly and maintain positive relationships.

F. Poor Performance:

- **Consequences:** Unspecified techniques may lead to subpar performance, affecting the functionality and longevity of the constructed facility.

- **Solutions:** Involve experts in the planning phase to assess and specify appropriate construction techniques. Conduct feasibility studies to ensure performance requirements are met. Regularly monitor and evaluate performance during construction.

G. Aesthetic Issues:

- **Consequences:** Lack of specification can result in aesthetic inconsistencies, impacting the visual appeal of the completed project.

- **Solutions:** Include aesthetic considerations in construction specifications. Provide visual references and engage architects and designers to ensure the desired aesthetic outcomes. Regularly review and address any deviations from the specified aesthetics.

Conclusion

In conclusion, providing the contractor with an audited construction manual, verified by a Project Management Consultant (PMC) auditor, proves to be a strategic approach to proactively manage quality and streamline processes. This method provides a reliable framework for the contractor, offering a standardized and audited set of procedures that significantly reduces the likelihood of unforeseen surprises or deviations from established quality standards. By aligning the contractor's work methods with the audited construction manual, the project benefits from enhanced transparency, minimized risks, and a more efficient and controlled construction process. This collaborative approach ensures that all stakeholders are on the same page, fostering a shared commitment to delivering a high-quality outcome in a structured and predictable manner.

Case Study (5) of Unspecified Construction Techniques

One of our prestigious clients, Mr. Sharad Gupta, is located in New Friends Colony, New Delhi. Two months after the completion of the brickwork, the architect visited the site and noticed that no band had been provided at the bottom of the brickwork. The architect planned to flush the skirting with the plaster, leading to the decision to dismantle the entire brickwork and perform the necessary rework.

CHAPTER-6

The Unseen Consequences of Improper Planning and Scheduling

"The Cost of Rushing:
Delhi's Lesson in Planning and Scheduling"

Story for Chapter 6

Within the lively streets of Delhi, there worked a contractor named Sameer who prided himself on his ability to complete projects quickly. Sameer often took on more projects than he could handle, believing that his efficiency would make up for any shortcomings in planning and scheduling.

One day, Sameer was tasked with building a new office complex. Eager to impress his clients, he promised to complete the project in record time. However, Sameer did not take the time to properly plan and schedule the project, believing that his experience would suffice.

As the construction progressed, the flaws in Sameer's approach became apparent. The project faced delays and cost overruns as Sameer struggled to coordinate with suppliers and manage his workforce effectively. The quality of work suffered, and the clients became increasingly frustrated.

In the end, the project was completed, but it it fell short of Sameer's expectations. The clients were unhappy with the delays and the quality of work, and Sameer's reputation took a hit. He realized too late that proper planning and scheduling were essential for the success of any project.

Sameer's story serves as a cautionary tale for all involved in construction projects. Rushing through planning and scheduling may seem like a shortcut, but the unseen consequences can be severe. It's important to take the time to plan properly, even if it means taking longer to complete the project. After all, in the end, quality and efficiency go hand in hand.

Improper Planning and Scheduling

A. **Project Delays:**

- **Consequences:** Inadequate planning can lead to unrealistic timelines and unforeseen challenges, resulting in project delays.

- **Solutions:** Conduct a thorough project analysis during the planning phase. Establish realistic timelines, account for potential obstacles, and incorporate buffer periods into the schedule.

B. **Resource Over allocation:**

- **Consequences:** Poor scheduling may lead to the inefficient allocation of resources, causing bottlenecks and hampering overall productivity.

- **Solutions:** Implement resource leveling techniques to distribute work evenly. Regularly monitor resource usage and adjust schedules to avoid over allocation.

C. **Increased Costs:**

- **Consequences:** Insufficient planning may result in budget overruns due to unexpected expenses, rework, or rushed procurement.

- **Solutions:** Conduct a comprehensive cost analysis in the planning phase. Incorporate contingency funds for unforeseen expenses. Regularly review and update the budget as needed.

D. **Quality Compromises:**

- **Consequences:** Rushed schedules and inadequate planning can compromise the quality of work, leading to defects and the need for rework.

- **Solutions:** Prioritize thorough planning to allocate sufficient time for each task. Implement quality control measures and inspections to catch issues early on.

E. **Increased Risk of Changes:**

- **Consequences:** Poor planning may lead to frequent changes in project scope, causing disruptions and impacting overall project stability.

- **Solutions:** Conduct a comprehensive risk assessment during the planning phase. Clearly define project scope and objectives. Minimize changes once the project is underway.

Key Solutions for Effective Planning and Scheduling

A. Thorough Project Analysis:

- **Solution:** Conduct a detailed analysis during the planning phase to identify potential challenges, risks, and resource requirements.

B. Realistic Timelines:

- **Solution:** Set achievable and realistic project timelines. Factor in uncertainties and allocate sufficient time for each task.

C. Resource Leveling:

- **Solution:** Implement resource leveling techniques to ensure a balanced and efficient allocation of resources throughout the project.

D. Comprehensive Cost Analysis:

- **Solution:** Conduct a thorough cost analysis, including potential risks and contingencies, to create a realistic budget.

E. Quality Control Measures:

- **Solution:** Prioritize quality by implementing thorough planning and scheduling, along with regular quality control measures to catch and address issues early.

F. Risk Assessment:

- **Solution:** Conduct a comprehensive risk assessment to identify potential changes and challenges. Develop strategies to mitigate risks.

G. Clear Communication Channels:

- **Solution:** Establish and maintain clear communication channels among team members. Hold regular meetings and utilize project management tools to facilitate communication.

H. Work-Life Balance:

- **Solution:** Prioritize the well-being of team members by setting realistic workloads, monitoring work hours, and promoting a healthy work-life balance.

I. Customer Expectation Management:

- **Solution:** Communicate transparently with customers, providing realistic timelines and progress updates. Address concerns promptly to manage expectations effectively.

Conclusion

In conclusion, the findings from Wellingtone underscore the widespread challenge of completing projects within budget, with 66% of companies reporting difficulties. The most common reasons for budget overruns include poor estimates, scope changes, inadequate budget management, project delays, improper risk management, and insufficient resource management.

Case Study (6) of The Unseen Consequences of Improper Planning and Scheduling

One of our colleagues worked on a warehouse project in Sonipat. The warehouse covers an area of around 10 acres, with the land sloping 3 meters down from the main road. The client initially planned to fill the lower area for future use and began construction. However, upon completing the construction, they faced challenges in immediately sourcing the required amount of soil for filling the lower land. As a result, the project is facing delays of almost 6 months due to this unavailability of soil.

The challenge underscores the critical importance of thorough planning and precise execution in project management. It highlights the need for careful foresight and strategic decision-making to anticipate potential obstacles and ensure the seamless progress of any undertaking. This experience serves as a valuable lesson in emphasizing the significance of comprehensive planning and efficient execution for the successful completion of projects.

Pitfalls of an Improperly Timed Procurement Schedule

Story for Chapter 7

A construction manager named Kunal was in charge of a new commercial complex being developed in the vibrant city of Kolkata. Despite his skill and experience, he underestimated the importance of timing in procurement.

As the project progressed, Kunal realized that his procurement schedule was not well-planned. He had ordered materials too early, leading to storage issues and increased costs. At the same time, he had delayed ordering some critical items, causing delays in the construction timeline.

These mistakes had a domino effect on the project. The delays meant that the contractors had to be paid for longer, stretching the project's overall budget thin. The quality of work also suffered, as the rushed schedule led to errors and rework.

Kunal knew he had to make changes. He worked closely with his team to create a detailed procurement schedule that aligned with the construction timeline. He also established better communication channels with suppliers to ensure timely delivery of materials.

Slowly but surely, the project started to get back on track. The materials were delivered on time, and construction progressed smoothly. In the end, the commercial complex was completed, albeit slightly behind schedule, but with a higher quality of workmanship.

Kunal's story reminds us of the importance of a well-planned procurement schedule. Timing is everything in construction, and a small delay in procurement can have far-reaching consequences. It's essential to take the time to plan properly and ensure that materials are ordered and delivered at the right time. After all, in construction, every day counts.

Pitfalls of an Improperly Timed Procurement Schedule:

A. Delayed Project Start:

- **Consequences:** An improperly timed procurement schedule can result in delays in acquiring necessary materials or services, causing a delayed project start.

- **Solutions:** Align the procurement schedule with the overall project timeline. Initiate procurement processes early, considering lead times and potential delays in the procurement cycle.

B. **Increased Project Costs:**

- **Consequences:** Delays in procurement may lead to increased costs due to rush orders, expedited shipping, or last-minute purchases at higher prices.

- **Solutions:** Develop a comprehensive procurement plan, accurately estimate lead times, and negotiate favorable terms with suppliers to minimize costs.

C. **Quality Compromises:**

- **Consequences:** Rushed procurement decisions can result in compromises on the quality of materials or services, impacting the overall project quality.

- **Solutions:** Put strict quality control procedures in place. Make early supplier involvement a priority in order to guarantee compliance with project requirements and standards.

D. **Contractual Disputes:**

- **Consequences:** An improperly timed procurement schedule can lead to disputes with suppliers over delivery times, terms, and conditions.

- **Solutions:** Clearly define expectations in procurement contracts. Regularly communicate with suppliers and address any issues promptly to prevent disputes.

E. **Limited Supplier Options:**

- **Consequences:** A rushed procurement schedule may limit the pool of available suppliers, reducing the ability to choose the most cost-effective and reliable options.

- **Solutions:** Start the procurement process early to allow for a thorough evaluation of potential suppliers, fostering better negotiation and selection processes.

F. **Inadequate Risk Management:**

- **Consequences:** Failure to account for potential risks in the procurement schedule can lead to disruptions, such as supply chain issues or unexpected delays.

- **Solutions:** Conduct a comprehensive risk assessment, identify potential procurement risks, and develop mitigation strategies. Regularly review and update risk management plans.

Key Solutions for Mitigating Pitfalls

A. Comprehensive Procurement Planning:

- **Solution:** Develop a detailed procurement plan aligned with the project timeline. Clearly outline procurement milestones and deadlines.

B. Early Supplier Engagement:

- **Solution:** Engage with suppliers early in the project lifecycle. Discuss project requirements, lead times, and expectations to ensure a collaborative and informed procurement process.

C. Accurate Lead Time Estimation:

- **Solution:** Conduct thorough research on lead times for materials or services. Factor in potential delays and uncertainties to create realistic timelines.

D. Negotiation and Contract Clarity:

- **Solution:** Negotiate favorable terms with suppliers, considering delivery times and pricing. Clearly define expectations and conditions in procurement contracts to avoid misunderstandings.

E. Continuous Communication:

- **Solution:** Maintain open and continuous communication with suppliers. Provide regular updates on project progress and be proactive in addressing any procurement-related issues.

F. Flexible Procurement Schedule:

- **Solution:** Design a procurement schedule that allows for flexibility to accommodate changes, unforeseen circumstances, or adjustments in project timelines.

G. Supplier Evaluation:

- **Solution:** Start the supplier evaluation process early to have a broader pool of options. Consider factors beyond cost, such as reliability, reputation, and track record.

H. Robust Risk Management:

- **Solution:** Conduct a thorough risk assessment for procurement activities. Develop contingency plans and regularly review and update them to address evolving project conditions.

By addressing these solutions, organizations can effectively manage the risks associated with improperly timed procurement schedules, ensuring smoother project execution, cost-effectiveness, and higher overall project quality.

Conclusion

In conclusion, one of the most important ways to shorten project durations and optimize project timeframes is to create a bar chart for the procurement calendar that clearly indicates major from minor items. Through the use of graphic representations of the procurement schedules for various item categories, stakeholders and project managers can identify possible bottlenecks and make targeted interventions to speed up important procurement procedures.

This approach aligns with the importance of early and effective procurement planning, emphasizing the need to prioritize major items while ensuring timely acquisition of minor items. The bar chart provides a visual roadmap that aids in resource allocation, risk management, and supplier engagement, ultimately contributing to a well-coordinated and efficient procurement strategy.

By leveraging the insights derived from this visual representation, project teams can proactively address challenges, negotiate favorable terms, and optimize the procurement schedule. This not only helps in preventing delays and cost overruns but also enhances the overall quality of project outcomes. The bar chart serves as a valuable tool for decision-makers to make informed choices, foster collaboration with suppliers, and successfully expedite the procurement process, thus contributing to the overarching goal of reducing project time.

Case Study (7) of Improperly Timed Procurement Schedule

We executed the interior work for a hostel building project for one of our clients, with an initial timeline of 6 months for completion. Remarkably, we were able to finish the project in just 4 months. However, an oversight occurred when we neglected to place an order for a specific aluminum window until after the completion of the main construction. Initially, we assumed the window would be delivered within 7-8 days; however, it turned out to be a specialized product imported from Germany, resulting in a 2-month delay in its arrival. This unforeseen circumstance led to a 2-month delay in the overall project timeline. This incident underscores the crucial importance of meticulous prior planning of procurement in project management.

CHAPTER-8

Dangers of an Undefined Financial Project Map

Story for Chapter 8

Rahul was a project manager supervising the building of a new factory in the industrial hub of Manesar. Rahul was confident in his abilities but overlooked the importance of having a well-defined financial project map.

As the project progressed, Rahul became aware of the many difficulties he was encountering in the absence of a well-defined financial plan. He was finding it difficult to keep track of costs as they increased. Additionally, there were delays in paying contractors, which caused construction to slow down.

These issues had a ripple effect on the project. Contractors became frustrated, and some even left the project midway. The quality of work suffered, as Rahul had to take shortcuts in order to stay under budget, which affected the quality of the work. The project's overall progress was impeded, and Rahul was put in a challenging position.

Determined to turn things around, Rahul decided to create a detailed financial project map. He carefully assessed all costs, including materials, labor, and overheads, and created a realistic budget. He also set up a system to track expenses and payments, ensuring that everything was in order.

The project gradually regained momentum. Contractors were paid on time, and the overall quality of work improved. The factory was completed within budget, but slightly behind schedule, and to a higher standard of workmanship.

Rahul's story serves as a helpful reminder of the importance of having a well-defined financial project map. Without a clear plan, projects can quickly spiral out of control. It's essential to take the time to create a detailed budget and financial plan to ensure the success of any project. After all, in construction, financial planning is key to success.

Undefined Financial Project Map

A. Budget Overruns:

- **Consequences:** Without a clearly defined financial project map, there is a risk of budget overruns due to unforeseen expenses and inadequate cost planning.

- **Solutions:** Develop a comprehensive financial project map that includes detailed budget estimates, contingency plans, and regular financial reviews to track and control expenses.

B. Poor Resource Allocation:

- **Consequences:** Lack of clarity in financial planning can lead to inefficient resource allocation, causing bottlenecks and hampering project progress.

- **Solutions:** Clearly outline resource requirements in the financial project map. Regularly review and adjust resource allocations based on project needs and priorities.

C. **Inadequate Risk Management:**

- **Consequences:** An undefined financial project map may result in insufficient risk management, leaving the project vulnerable to financial uncertainties.

- **Solutions:** Incorporate a risk management plan into the financial project map. Identify potential financial risks, develop mitigation strategies, and regularly reassess and update the risk management plan.

Key Solutions for Mitigating Risks

A. **Comprehensive Financial Project Map:**

- **Solution:** Develop a detailed financial project map that includes budget estimates, resource requirements, and a breakdown of expenses across project phases.

B. **Detailed Budget Estimates:**

- **Solution:** Conduct thorough research and analysis to create accurate budget estimates. Consider potential risks and uncertainties to ensure the budget is realistic and comprehensive.

C. **Regular Financial Reviews:**

- **Solution:** Implement a schedule for regular financial reviews throughout the project lifecycle. Evaluate actual expenditures against the budget and adjust financial plans accordingly.

D. Transparency with Stakeholders:

- **Solution:** Foster open communication with stakeholders. Clearly communicate financial decisions, involve stakeholders in the planning process, and address concerns promptly to maintain trust and collaboration.

By implementing these solutions, organizations can mitigate the dangers associated with an unclear financial project map. A clearly defined and actively managed financial plan provides a roadmap for project success, helping to control costs, allocate resources efficiently, and navigate potential financial challenges effectively.

Conclusion

In conclusion, creating a bar chart to outline projected expenses, similar to a work bar chart, is a vital component for effective project financial management. This visual representation provides a clear and accessible overview of anticipated expenses across different project phases, mirroring the structure of a work breakdown structure (WBS). By aligning financial planning with project activities, the bar chart enables project managers and stakeholders to identify, prioritize, and allocate resources efficiently, reducing the risks associated with budget overruns, poor resource allocation, and inadequate risk management.

Much like a work bar chart facilitates the tracking of project progress, a required expenses bar chart serves as a dynamic tool for monitoring and controlling financial aspects of the project. It encourages proactive decision-making, facilitates transparency, and aids in the prevention of scope creep and stakeholder disputes. The bar chart becomes an essential guide for project teams, offering a visual roadmap to navigate the complexities of financial planning and ensuring that expenses align with project objectives. Ultimately, the integration of a required expenses bar chart enhances financial project management, contributing to the overall success and sustainability of the project.

○ ○ ○ ○

Case Study (8) of Dangers of an Undefined Financial Project Map

One of our clients in Manesar, Haryana, was in the process of constructing a factory, and their initial budget for the project was set at 3.5 crore. However, as the work commenced, the budget escalated, ultimately reaching 4.5 crore. Unfortunately, they were unable to arrange an additional 1 crore, resulting in the incomplete realization of their factory project. Consequently, they had to sell the partially constructed facility. This situation emphasizes the importance of having a precise understanding of the actual costs involved in a project. Had the client been aware of the true costs beforehand, they might have reconsidered initiating the project, thereby avoiding financial setbacks and incomplete construction.

Connecting Success through Full-Spectrum Kitting

Story for Chapter 9

In the heart of Haryana, there was a construction foreman named Deepak who was known for his meticulous planning and attention to detail. Deepak understood the importance of full-spectrum kitting in construction projects and the impact it could have on the success of a project.

One day, Deepak got put in charge of building a new office building. The project was complex, with multiple components that needed to come together seamlessly. Deepak knew that full-spectrum kitting would be crucial in ensuring that everything ran smoothly.

So, Deepak took the time to carefully plan and organize the project's materials and supplies. He made sure that everything was ordered and delivered on time, and that all the necessary tools and equipment were readily available. He also worked closely with his team to ensure that everyone understood their roles and responsibilities.

As the project progressed, Deepak's attention to detail paid off. The construction site was well-organized, and work progressed smoothly. There were no delays due to missing materials or equipment, and the project was completed on time and within budget.

The success of the project was a testament to the power of full-spectrum kitting. Deepak's careful planning and preparation had ensured that everything ran smoothly, and the project was a success.

Deepak's story serves as a reminder of the importance of full-spectrum kitting in construction projects. By taking the time to plan and organize materials and supplies, construction teams can ensure that everything runs smoothly and that projects are completed successfully. After all, in construction, preparation is key to success.

Connecting Success through Full Spectrum Kitting Solutions

A. Enhanced Efficiency:

- **Details:** Full spectrum kitting involves the strategic grouping of components and materials required for specific tasks or projects. This streamlines processes by ensuring that all necessary items are readily available, minimizing time spent searching for and gathering materials.

- **Impact:** Improved efficiency leads to faster project completion, reduced downtime, and increased overall productivity.

B. **Inventory Optimization:**

- **Details:** Full spectrum kitting enables better control over inventory by creating pre-assembled kits with the exact quantities needed. This helps in reducing excess stock, preventing shortages, and facilitating accurate demand forecasting.

- **Impact:** Cost savings are achieved through reduced holding costs, minimized waste, and optimized use of storage space.

C. **Error Reduction:**

- **Details:** By preassembling kits with carefully curated components, the likelihood of errors or missing items is significantly reduced. This ensures that workers have everything they need for a particular task, eliminating the need for last-minute adjustments or substitutions.

- **Impact:** Improved accuracy, decreased rework, and enhanced product or project quality are achieved.

D. **Streamlined Procurement:**

- **Details:** Full spectrum kitting involves a comprehensive approach to procurement, ensuring that all necessary components are sourced and organized in advance. This minimizes the risk of procurement delays and enables better negotiation with suppliers.

- **Impact:** Timely availability of materials, reduced procurement costs, and increased negotiation leverage result.

E. Task Standardization:

- **Details:** Through full spectrum kitting, organizations can standardize tasks by providing workers with pre-defined sets of tools and materials for specific activities. This fosters consistency in processes and outcomes.

- **Impact:** Consistent quality, reduced variability, and easier training of new team members are facilitated.

F. Time and Cost Savings:

- **Details:** Full spectrum kitting saves valuable time by eliminating the need for workers to search for and gather materials. Additionally, the optimized procurement and inventory management result in cost savings.

- **Impact:** Reduced labor costs, faster project completion, and improved overall project profitability are realized.

G. Flexibility and Adaptability:

- **Details:** Full spectrum kitting allows for flexibility in adjusting kits based on evolving project requirements. This adaptability ensures that teams have the right tools and materials, even in dynamic or changing work environments.

- **Impact:** Improved responsiveness to changing project needs, enhanced agility, and the ability to address unexpected challenges are provided.

H. Worker Satisfaction:

- **Details:** Providing workers with well-organized kits that contain all the necessary tools and materials contributes to a positive work environment. This, in turn, boosts morale and job satisfaction.

- **Impact:** Increased employee engagement, lower turnover rates, and a more positive workplace culture are fostered.

I. Traceability and Accountability:

- **Details:** Full spectrum kitting allows for better traceability of materials used in each kit. This enhances accountability, as it becomes easier to track usage, identify potential issues, and allocate costs accurately.

- **Impact:** Improved financial transparency, better decision-making, and effective cost control are achieved.

J. Sustainable Practices:

- **Details:** By optimizing inventory and reducing waste through full spectrum kitting, organizations contribute to sustainable practices. This aligns with environmental and corporate social responsibility goals.

- **Impact:** Enhanced corporate reputation, compliance with sustainability standards, and reduced environmental impact.

Conclusion

In conclusion, the concept of Full Spectrum Kitting serves as a transformative strategy, connecting success across various dimensions of project and operational management. By seamlessly integrating efficiency, inventory optimization, error reduction, streamlined procurement, task standardization, time and cost savings, flexibility, worker satisfaction, traceability, and sustainable practices, Full Spectrum Kitting becomes a cornerstone for organizations aspiring to achieve holistic success. This approach not only enhances productivity and project outcomes but also contributes to a positive work environment, financial transparency, and sustainable business practices. Overall, Full Spectrum Kitting offers so many benefits that it's essential for organizations wanting to do well in today's fast-paced and competitive world.

Case Study (9) of Connecting Success through Full-Spectrum Kitting

Whenever we start a new project, it's crucial to pay attention to small details and make necessary arrangements in advance. Once, during doing concrete casting for a rooftop at Mount Carmel School in Dwarka, our vibrator broke, and unfortunately, we couldn't arrange a replacement in time due to the late hour—it was approximately 1.30AM. This resulted in the wastage of 30 cubic meters of concrete, causing significant financial losses and delays. This incident highlights the importance of planning and ensuring the availability of essential equipment to avoid such issues during project execution. Therefore, we have to make the full kitting list according to activity.

CHAPTER-10

Costly Consequences of Delayed Contractor Payments

Story for Chapter 10

In Noida's lively setting, there worked a construction project manager named Alok who was overseeing the construction of a new residential building. Alok was diligent in his work but underestimated the impact of delayed contractor payments.

As the project progressed, Alok found himself facing delays in payments to contractors. He believed that these delays were unavoidable and did not realize the costly consequences they would have on the project.

The delays in payments started to take a toll on the project. Contractors became frustrated and demotivated, leading to a slowdown in construction. Some contractors even left the project midway, causing further delays and complications.

These setbacks set off a chain reaction. The delays led to increased costs, as contractors had to be paid for longer periods. The quality of work suffered, as the project was rushed to meet deadlines. In the end, the project was completed, but it was behind schedule and over budget.

Alok realized his mistake and vowed to do better in the future. He understood the importance of timely contractor payments and the impact they could have on the success of a project. He made changes to his payment process, ensuring that contractors were paid on time and that communication lines were kept open.

Alok's story stands as a powerful reminder of the importance of timely contractor payments in construction projects. Delayed payments can have costly consequences, leading to delays, increased costs, and lower quality of work. Therefore, it's essential to prioritize timely payments to ensure the success of any project.

Consequences of Delayed Contractor Payment

A. Strained Contractor Relationships:

- **Consequences:** Delayed payments strain relationships with contractors, leading to dissatisfaction and potential disputes. This may result in reluctance to work on future projects or a decline in the quality of work.

B. Decreased Productivity:

- **Consequences:** Contractors may prioritize projects that offer timely payments, leading to delays in ongoing projects. This decreased productivity can result in project setbacks and increased costs.

C. Legal Implications:

- **Consequences:** Delayed payments may trigger legal disputes and contractual breaches. Contractors may take legal action to recover payments, resulting in legal fees, fines, and damage to the reputation of the hiring organization.

D. Higher Project Costs:

- **Consequences:** Late payments can lead to contractors increasing their rates to compensate for financial uncertainties, ultimately increasing the overall cost of projects.

E. Impact on Subcontractors and Suppliers:

- **Consequences:** Delayed payments to contractors can cascade into payment delays for subcontractors and suppliers. This can disrupt the entire supply chain, affecting project timelines and quality.

F. Quality of Work Compromises:

- **Consequences:** Contractors facing financial strain may cut corners or compromise on the quality of work to compensate for delayed payments, leading to subpar project outcomes.

G. Reduced Contractor Motivation:

Consequences: Contractors, demotivated by delayed payments, may lose interest in delivering high-quality work. This can result in a lack of commitment, affecting project timelines and outcomes.

Key Solutions to Mitigate the Consequences

A. Timely Invoice Processing:

- **Solution:** Implement efficient invoice processing systems to ensure timely verification and approval. Streamlining payment processes reduces the likelihood of delays.

B. Clear Payment Terms in Contracts:

- **Solution:** Clearly define payment terms in contracts, including due dates and any applicable penalties for late payments. This sets clear expectations and consequences.

C. Transparent Communication:

- **Solution:** Maintain open and transparent communication with contractors regarding payment schedules. Inform them promptly of any potential delays and work collaboratively to find solutions.

D. Automated Payment Systems:

- **Solution:** Implement automated payment systems to expedite the payment process. This reduces the likelihood of human errors and ensures consistency in payment timelines.

E. Financial Planning and Budgeting:

- **Solution:** Plan and budget adequately for contractor payments, considering cash flow and project milestones. Robust financial planning minimizes the risk of unexpected delays.

F. **Early Payment Discounts:**

- **Solution:** Encourage prompt payments by offering early payment discounts to contractors. This provides an incentive for timely completion of projects and adherence to payment schedules.

G. **Regular Performance Reviews:**

- **Solution:** Conduct regular performance reviews and assessments of contractors. Recognize and reward timely and high-quality work, fostering a positive working relationship.

H. **Contingency Funds:**

- **Solution:** Maintain contingency funds to address unexpected financial challenges or delays. This ensures that payments can be made promptly even in unforeseen circumstances.

I. **Supplier Financing Programs:**

- **Solution:** Establish supplier financing programs that allow contractors to access financing options, reducing financial strain and mitigating the impact of delayed payments.

In summary, addressing the consequences of delayed contractor payment requires a multifaceted approach involving streamlined processes, clear communication, financial planning, and collaboration. Implementing these solutions not only mitigates the negative impacts on relationships, project timelines, and costs but also fosters a positive and collaborative environment for successful project outcomes.

Conclusion

In conclusion, adopting a pre-billing system that matches the total estimation with the billing format offers a proactive approach to address delays in contractor payments. By incorporating a flexible billing cycle based on the work completed, such as the agreement to pay Rs. 25 lakhs within 2 to 3 days of the executed quantity, organizations can ensure timely and transparent payments to contractors. This system not only promotes a smoother workflow during construction but also enhances collaboration and trust between parties. The emphasis on real-time quantity checks and immediate payments aligns financial processes with project progress, creating an environment conducive to timely and efficient project completion. Overall, the pre-billing system proves to be a valuable strategy for avoiding payment delays and optimizing the construction project's financial management.

Case Study (10) of Costly Consequences of Delayed Contractor Payment

It is a common practice to delay payments to contractors, but this isn't recommended. Timely payments can improve a contractor's effectiveness as they often have financial limitations. For instance, during the construction of a commercial building in Gurgaon with a project cost of Rs.25 Crore, the owner met with contractors and selected one. They discussed the billing cycle, and the contractor suggested a standard 14-day cycle.

The owner proposed a quicker payment release within 24 hours of invoicing, offering a 2% discount, amounting to Rs.50 Lakh. To facilitate this, the owner implemented a pre-billing system, creating a detailed bill format with input from engineers on both sides to track daily quantities of work done. These quantities were multiplied by the rates, and as soon as the billing reached Rs.50 Lakh, the owner promptly released the payment.

This procedure allowed the contractor to make cash purchases for necessary items, taking advantage of 2% to 3% discounts from suppliers. This efficient payment system proved beneficial for both parties involved.

Unleashing the Power of Checklists and Construction Manuals in Project Excellence

Story for Chapter 11

In the vibrant city of Greater Noida, there resided Ravi, a construction manager renowned for his attention to detail and commitment to excellence. Ravi understood the power of checklists and construction manuals in ensuring the success of a project.

One day, he was assigned to supervise the construction of a new shopping complex. The project was ambitious, with tight deadlines and high expectations. Ravi knew that he needed to have a solid plan in place to ensure that everything ran smoothly.

Ravi decided to create a detailed checklist and construction manual for the project. He meticulously outlined each step of the construction process, from site preparation to final inspections. He also included safety protocols and quality control measures to ensure that the project met all standards and regulations.

As the project progressed, Ravi's checklists and construction manuals proved to be invaluable. They helped keep the project on track, ensuring that all tasks were completed on time and to the highest standards. They also served as a guide for his team, helping them understand their roles and responsibilities.

Thanks to Ravi's foresight and planning, the shopping complex stood tall within the stipulated timeframe and budget. The quality of work was exceptional, and the project was hailed as a success.

Ravi's story underscores the significance of checklists and construction manuals in achieving project excellence. By taking the time to create detailed plans and guidelines, construction managers can ensure that their projects are successful and meet all expectations. After all, in construction, careful planning is the key to building dreams.

Power of Checklists

A. Enhanced Quality Assurance:

- **Benefits:** Checklists and construction manuals provide a systematic and comprehensive guide for project activities, ensuring that each task is executed according to predetermined standards. This leads to improved quality assurance, reducing the likelihood of errors and rework.

B. Standardized Processes:

- **Benefits:** Checklists and construction manuals establish standardized processes for various construction activities. This consistency promotes efficiency, streamlines operations, and enables seamless collaboration among project teams.

C. Improved Communication:

- **Benefits:** Clear and detailed checklists and construction manuals facilitate effective communication among project stakeholders. This ensures that everyone is on the same page regarding project requirements, methodologies, and quality standards.

D. Efficient Resource Utilization:

- Benefits: Checklists and construction manuals help optimize resource allocation by providing a detailed roadmap for each activity. This minimizes the risk of resource wastage, prevents over allocation, and contributes to cost-effective project management.

E. Mitigation of Risks:

- **Benefits:** Construction manuals include guidelines for risk management, helping project teams identify potential risks and implement mitigation strategies. Checklists ensure that these risk management measures are systematically addressed, reducing the impact of unforeseen challenges.

F. Accelerated Learning Curve:

- **Benefits:** Checklists and construction manuals serve as valuable training tools for new team members. The detailed documentation speeds up the learning process, helping newcomers grasp project processes and requirements more rapidly.

G. Enhanced Project Control:

- **Benefits:** The use of checklists and construction manuals provides project managers with a greater degree of control over project activities. This empowers them to monitor progress, identify deviations, and take corrective actions promptly.

H. Time and Cost Savings:

- **Benefits:** Standardized processes and efficient resource utilization contribute to time and cost savings. The clarity provided by checklists and construction manuals reduces the likelihood of delays, rework, and unexpected expenses.

I. Improved Stakeholder Confidence:

- **Benefits:** By consistently following checklists and construction manuals, project stakeholders such as clients, investors, and regulatory bodies gain confidence. The transparent and standardized approach enhances the project's reputation and credibility.

J. Facilitation of Continuous Improvement:

- **Benefits:** Checklists and construction manuals create a foundation for continuous improvement. Regular reviews and updates to these documents allow project teams to incorporate lessons learned, industry best practices, and emerging standards, ensuring ongoing project excellence.

H. Increased Accountability:

- **Benefits:** The use of checklists and construction manuals fosters accountability among team members. With clearly defined tasks and expectations, individuals are more likely to take ownership of their responsibilities, reducing the risk of oversights.

I. Client Satisfaction:

- **Benefits:** Meeting client expectations by delivering high-quality projects on time and within budget is essential for client satisfaction. Checklists and construction manuals play a crucial role in achieving these outcomes, leading to positive feedback and potential future collaborations.

Conclusion

In conclusion, the power of checklists and construction manuals in project excellence lies in their ability to establish standardized processes, enhance communication, mitigate risks, optimize resource utilization, and facilitate continuous improvement. These tools not only contribute to the efficient execution of projects but also foster a culture of quality, accountability, and client satisfaction, ultimately leading to the overall success of construction endeavors.

Case Study (11) of Power of Checklists and Construction Manuals in Project Excellence

83

In every project, we've used checklists to make sure our work is top-notch, and it's made a huge difference, cutting mistakes by 90%. Whether it's building a house or a big building, these checklists have been our go-to, helping us double-check every little thing

Call to Action

As we reach the end of this book, I would like to express my deepest gratitude for taking the time to read "11 MOST COMMON MISTAKES WHICH INCREASE COST AND TIME AND DECREASES THE QUALITY OF CONSTRUCTION."

Your feedback is invaluable and could greatly benefit others exploring this resource. If you've found insights or have questions to share, please do! Your input can make a big difference for someone else. Additionally, if you have any queries or need suggestions for your upcoming project, simply scan the barcode and reach out to us.

We're here to help you succeed. Thank you!

If you want to download the free construction checklist manual, you can scan the barcode and contact us.